AF438325

Gonbad-e Qabus (ca. mid 20th century)

**EASTERN
STRUCTURES**

editor

R. W. Watkins

creative consultants

Jim Wilson
Jacqueline Jones

printing / production

Nocturnal Iris
World Headquarters
in conjunction with KDP
and Amazon.com

Cover, page 2 and above:
Gonbad-e Qabus (built 1006-07
AD), Gonbad-e Kavus, Iran

Eastern Structures is published
four times a year by
Nocturnal Iris Publications

PO Box 111
Moreton's Harbour, NL
A0G 3H0 Canada

Postal submissions of poems, essays,
reviews or related material should be
accompanied by an SASE (in Canada) or
an SAE + IRC (outside of Canada).
Electronic submissions should be e-
mailed to nocturnaliris@gmail.com.

EASTERN STRUCTURES

Number 22 • Spring/Summer, 2022 • ISBN: 9798848401646

CONTENTS

4   forward
28   about the contributors

e s s a y s

22   'Haiku Mind, Enlightenment, and R. H. Blyth': Three related
essays by Jim Wilson

t h e   p o e m s

Anum, Faiza...p. 5
Aylett, Jonathan...pp. 18, 19 and 27
Baglow, John...pp. 5, 6 and 17
Burton, Marcia..p. 18
Gibb, E. J. W...pp. 9 and 10
Hepworth, Reid...p. 20
Hosseini, Mace..p. 7
Leaf, Walter...pp. 11 and 12
Lignori, James..p. 27
Lubman, Alex...pp. 18, 20 and 21
Mangan, James Clarence..................................pp. 15 and 16
Parker, G. C..p. 18
Payne, John...pp. 13 and 14
Shahrukh, J. F...p. 8
St. Claire, Joshua...........................pp. 18, 19, 20 and 27
Stone, Alison...p. 7
Watkins, R. W...pp. 19 and 21
Woerner, Danielle...pp. 19, 20 and 27
Writer-Davies, Gareth...p. 17
Zwinger, Lynda...pp. 19, 20 and 21

Page 9: portrait of Suleiman the Magnificent (ca. 1530) reputedly by Titian
Page 16: portrait of J. C. Mangan after death (1849) by Frederic W. Burton

Forward

What if I were to tell you that, contrary to popular belief, numerous Western poets translated Persian ghazals into the English language between the late eighteenth and the early twentieth centuries, preserving elements like qafia and radif in the process? What would you think? What if you were to make such an inadvertent discovery in your research? What do you do with information like that?

Informed of what I'd unearthed, long-time haiku poet and editor Jim Wilson commented that such a situation reminds him of his discovery of so many formal (5-7-5) haiku written in the early decades of the twentieth century.

"The sidelining of treasure troves of formal haiku and formal ghazal is part of the story of how free verse has become normative," observed Wilson. "In the case of ghazal, I think it can be understood as a kind of cultural imperialism. That's difficult for free-verse people to look at because they tend to see themselves as progressives rather than colonials. But free verse is a specifically Western cultural creation, and when it undermines other poetic cultures it plays a colonial role. Perhaps that interpretation is too political, and a better way of looking at it is what I call the hegemonic tendency of free verse."

It's perfectly fine for Wilson to compare such anomalous discoveries to conveniently forgotten haiku—he's by no means wrong in his observations. But here's where the matter becomes problematic on a level different from what we've been accustomed to seeing in the haiku world:

In the introduction to his 2000 anthology *Ravishing DisUnities: Real Ghazals in English*, formal ghazal advocate Agha Shahid Ali makes mention of early instances of the form in English—quoting late nineteenth and early twentieth century examples by James Clarence Mangan and James Elroy Flecker in their entireties. In that same intro, Ali claims that "while translating an Urdu or Persian ghazal into English, one would have to use free verse (it would be impossible to sustain a convincing qafia—given the radif—when translating couplet after couplet; however, Andrew McCord in his translation of Ghalib in this anthology may well be proving me wrong)." Is it possible that a Kashmiri-American literary scholar was aware of such anomalous originals as the Mangan and Flecker poems but not John Payne's three-volume monorhyme translations of Hafez? Is it conceivable that he was not aware of similar translations by the likes of E. J. W. Gibb, R. A. Nicholson and Walter Leaf?

Jim Wilson insists that it is possible that Ali was completely unaware of these earlier translations, owing to the success of free-verse advocates at "casting these kinds of efforts into a shadowy past that is difficult to access".

Yes, it *is* indeed possible. Matters are not helped by the fact that such early translators usually referred to such poems as *odes*; and that on those rare occasions when they did refer to them as *ghazals*, they usually wrote the term as *ghazel* or *gazel*. Either way, it wasn't something that was going to readily deliver relevant search results on a 1990s web browser. Still, I must note in the way of argument, I somehow managed to stumble upon a R. A. Nicholson translation in my final year of high school, in that pre-Internet 'dark age' of nearly three and a half decades ago.

Wilson also suggested the possibility that Ali's "sensitivity to imperialism might have created a barrier to accessing these earlier translators" if he viewed them as representative of the British Empire.

That's also quite possible. However, I must point out that several of the early translators spent considerable time in the countries of the ghazal's native tongues, where they were highly respected as purveyors of Eastern culture. In fact, when Edward G. Browne died in 1926, his passing was marked in Persia with a public day of mourning.

We must also face the possibility that such early translators were quite anomalous in the smooth course of history upon which Ali wished to make an impact. They were something of an affront to him—a reminder of his admitted inability to preserve the ghazal's form when translating Faiz Ahmed Faiz (*The Rebel's Silhouette*, 1992). After all, he was only human.

Seriously, this may have all sorts of ramifications in regards to Ali's impact on ghazal history, depending on how we interpret his non-acknowledgement of the early British translators. For the moment, however, let us focus on the verse and prose contained in this issue; including a selection of ghazals—both original poems and translations of Persian classics—from *Early Journeys, Forgotten Logs*, my recently compiled anthology of ancient examples of the form in English. Believe me, there's still a lot to be learned from these old British and Irish pioneers—even when some of them were not completely clear on the attributes of the form in which they were working. Invariably, it pays to explore the explorers and their explorations. Enjoy.

R. W. Watkins

Ukraine from Ottawa

John Baglow

Horizon, shrouding a glow in the dark.
Night within night, what will grow in the dark?

The moon's expenditure. So weary, now,
feasting on flesh. Cold winds blow in the dark.

Reports echo. Blind, groping, soon enough
we learn what skeletons sow in the dark.

All of us are waging war in our way,
reaping a harvest of snow in the dark.

It's getting late. Windows are mirrors now.
We are consoled: blood will flow in the dark.

John can barely see your face, so long past
his love. Knowing what we know in the dark.

Ghazal: My Heart

Faiza Anum

Do not open for visits; let it stay hushed – my heart!
The mausoleum of your memory crushed my heart!

Look! How the trees submitted to the calls of the wind!
My portion of grief and regret is yet shushed – my heart!

How I discovered a geography to map stories we never lived;
"My face was the last metaphor in his eyes," gushed my heart!

In search of epiphanies, I light clay lamps in the charcoal nights.
Unable to reach your hands, my tears falling on tar – rushed, my heart!

With every rain, my eyes change colours like the sky.
Purple purple is the angst, and red-blushed, my heart!

Moist – the desire of reunion blooms out of my skin pores.
This spring is sterile – no leaves, no love – and bushed, my heart!

P.C.

John Baglow

What slipped through that wicked wire to the heart?
What set such a monstrous fire to the heart?

Years without quench. Your body spread out on
a scalding sea plumbs desire to the heart.

What exquisite shapes we carved in the dark,
what epics whispered entire to the heart!

Trails are soon overgrown in the wild spring,
meltwater flowing through mire to the heart.

Old maps mark our crumbling destinations
and memory is a liar to the heart.

John always ran towards lightning. Bright wisps catch
the edge of his mind, retire to the heart.

Cherry

Mace Hosseini

It's spring again; they dressed up the cherry tree, the pride in the orchard.
        She is given the veil of the blossoms; she's the bride in the orchard.

The garden is throwing bees on her, like the rice over newlyweds;
        The trees looking sharp, as if everyone's hair is dyed, in the orchard.

The summer comes, the veil is removed; the cherry is carrying fruit.
        She is blushed like glowing mothers-to-be that abide in the orchard.

Within her fruits she carries the seeds of her kind, more brides yet to come.
        She is quite concerned, because last summer many dried in the orchard.

She does what she needs to do, nurturing the fruits to the ripened state.
        She then lets go of the ruby rings, where others cried in the orchard.

She's alone again, having fed the bees, the birds and the gardener.
        She's facing the autumn of her life, like others tried in the orchard.

The sunshine subsides in density, the green leaves return to before;
        The rainbow leaves falling with the breeze—nowhere to hide—in the orchard.

Soon the bride is naked, lost of its innocence, covered with snow sheets.
        Winter has come to the garden. Our lady has died in the orchard.

That Month

Alison Stone

Wrists bound with satin cords, they wed in June.
Till death or an affair, he said in June.

Moon-fuelled, she keeps each man a month, shows her
faces to Caleb in May, Ted in June.

Sweet as pie in Anita Bryant's face,
dreams stored inside of poppies, red in June.

When rocket turns to bomb, we grieve in tribes.
Will there be peace or more bloodshed in June?

Downgraded from tornado, still the storm
rattles glass. Record heat ahead in June.

Rainbows fill store windows. Whatever sells.
The model poses on a sled in June.

Scared of cliché, she cuts spoons and the moon
from odes to ecstasy in bed in June.

Marie Kondo's for winter. Embrace mess.
Who wants boxes of bills to shred in June?

Resentments whistle to a boil. Long
mismatched marriage on its deathbed in June.

He cracked Nazi code, was convicted for
sex. Toast to Alan Turing – dead in June.

Flowers' gaudy colors beckon – *Stone, write
about us, not a man who fled in June.*

Ghazal

J. F. Shahrukh

perhaps, if i get to know you all the more
i'll know myself a little more

sometimes you and i cross paths at open doors
and my *self* yearns for love from before

you see through my scars and the plight of my woes
but yours i know you won't be able to score

i wish your life hadn't put you in throes
do you look at clouds and the edge of the shore?

perhaps, if my name wasn't bound to yours
i would've forgotten myself a little more

Gazel

Muhibbi (Sultan Suleiman I; 1494–1566)
Translated by E. J. W. Gibb

My pain for thee balm in my sight resembles;
Thy face's beam the clear moonlight resembles.
Thy black hair spread across thy cheeks, the roses,
O Liege, the garden's basil quite resembles.
Beside thy lip oped wide its mouth, the rosebud;
For shame it blushed, it blood outright resembles.
Thy mouth, a casket fair of pearls and rubies,
Thy teeth, pearls, thy lip coral bright resembles:
Their diver I, each morning and each even;
My weeping, Liege, the ocean's might resembles.
Lest he seduce thee, this my dread and terror,
That rival who Iblis in spite resembles. [1]
Around the taper bright, thy cheek, Muhibbi
Turns, and the moth in his sad plight resembles. [2]

(1882)

Suleiman the Magnificent

[1] *Iblis* is the Muslim name for Satan. The word is probably the same as *Diabolus*.
[2] The moth's love for the taper is a constant theme with Asian poets. The moth is a truer lover than even the nightingale; for, whereas the latter tells its love and its woes to all the world, the former, without a sigh, perishes in its beloved flame.

Gazel (from his *Mihnet-Keshan*[1])

'Izzet Molla (Kececizade Izzet Molla; 1786–1829)
Translated by E. J. W. Gibb

E. J. W. Gibb's translations of Muhibbi and Molla collected in *Early Journeys, Forgotten Logs:
The Nocturnal Iris Anthology of Ancient Ghazals in English* (2022); edited by R. W. Watkins.

After old rags longing hath the figure tall and slight of Love?
Fresh and fresh renews itself aye the brocade fire-bright of Love.
'Gainst the flames from thorns and thistles ne'er a curtain can be wove,
Nor 'neath honor's veil can hide the public shame, the blight of Love.
Through a needle's eye it sometimes vieweth far-off Hindustan—
Blind anon in its own country is the piercing sight of Love.
It will turn it to a ruin where naught save the owl may dwell,
In a home should chance be set the erring foot of plight of Love.
Will a single spark a hundred thousand homes consume at times:
One to me are both the highest and the lowest site of Love.
Never saw I one who knoweth—O most ignorant am I!
Yet doth each one vainly deem himself a learned wight in Love.
Rent and shattered—laid in ruins—all my caution's fortress vast
Have my evil Fate, my heart's black grain, the rage, the blight of Love. [2]
In its hell alike it tortures Musulman and infidel,
'Izzet, is there chance of freedom from its pangs, this plight of love?
Of reality hath made aware the seeker after Truth,
Showing lessons metaphoric, He, the Teacher bright St. Love!

(1882)

'Izzet Molla

---

[1] The *Mihnet Keshan* is a long poem of about 7,000 couplets. The name may be read "The
Sufferer," "The Sufferers," or "The Suffering of (at) Keshan." The town of Keshan was the scene of
the author's banishment.

[2] The seed, or grain of the heart, the heart's core—said to be the principle of life, or the sign of
original sin.

"

XIX

Hafiz (1325–1390)
Translated by Walter Leaf

Come back, my Saki, come; for of love-service fain am I,
Fate's suppliant, athirst to be bowed 'neath the chain am I.

Where through the radiant East of the wine-bowl thy glory dawns.
Rise, light my path; bewildered in life's mazes vain am I.

What though the surge of sin be about me to whelm me o'er?
Love's hand shall bear me up; his elect, purged of stain, am I.

Flout not the toper's call nor his ill name, O man of law;
What thing soe'er the counsels of God foreordain am I.

Drink wine; nor wealth nor will shall avail man the gift of love;
Heir since creation's dawn to the one golden gain am I.

What though afar I dwell in the flesh, far from peace and thee;
Natheless in heart and soul in thy court 'mid the train am I.

I who from land and home never yet wandered forth abroad,
Fain, but to see thy face, of the wild wave and plain am I.

Stand hills and seas between us; arise, Angel Guard, to aid;
Guide thou my steps; a weakling aghast, racked of pain am I.

West Wind, if e'er thou breathe of my love's ringlet musky sweet,
West Wind, beware, for jealousy's right hand insane am I.

Hafiz beneath thy footstep is yearning to yield his soul;
While life abides, the thrall of my heart's suzerain am I.

(1898)

XXI

Hafiz (1325–1390)
Translated by Walter Leaf

Though he wound me, yet he healeth therewithal;
His my soul is, his my life-breath therewithal.

Lo, the charm unnamed surpasseth favour fair;
Fair of face my love, and charmeth therewithal.

Either world is but the radiance round his head;
This my voice saith low, and loud saith therewithal.

Yea, my friends, though 'neath a veil I speak apart.
Yet my word world-wide resoundeth therewithal.

'Tis that eye-glance drunk with love spills all my blood,
'Tis that hair unbound that deals death therewithal.

Bear in mind how Love my heart hath sought to pierce.
Law despiseth, treaty breaketh therewithal.

Though fruition's nightly joys all pass away,
Yet desire's day dreary passeth therewithal.

On the world and world's delights set not the heart,
Nor the restless sky that rolleth therewithal.

All alike we quit the old world, one by one;
Beggar dieth, Sultan dieth therewithal.

He that wins love fears no judge; fill high the bowl;
Not the Sultan's doom he feareth therewithal;

Since the reeve knows well that Hafiz lives for love,
And the Wise King's Asaph knoweth therewithal.

(1898)

CCIV

Hafiz (1325–1390) / Translated by John Payne

The rose is come and best in Spring abideth
That in thy hand, save wine, no thing abideth.

Seize thou the hour; drink wine amid the roses,
For but a week their blossoming abideth.

Use, use the time of pleasance, for not always
A pearl in every oysterling abideth.

Rare way of love, where he his head uplifteth,
With whom no head, for love-liking abideth! [1]

Leave books, an thou wilt be our fellow student,
For Love's lore not in book-learning abideth.

Give ear and set thy heart on one whose beauty
In need of no bedizening abideth.

Come to our winehouse, elder, and a nectar
Quaff, such as not in Kauther's spring abideth.

Thou, who fill'st gold with rubies,[2] oh largesse him
With whom no gold, poor scatterling, abideth!

Grant me, o Lord, a draught without crop-sickness,
Wherein no headache for a sting abideth.

'Fore God I have a silver-bodied idol;[3]
In Terah's[4] joss-house no such thing abideth.

With all my heart, I'm Shah Uwéis's[4] bondman,
Of slaves unmindful though the King abideth[5]

The sun, —by his world-bright'ning cap I swear it, —
Than he less crown-embellishing abideth!

Those only carp and jibe at Hafiz' verses
In whom no grace of love-liking abideth.

(1901)

---

[1] The more a lover abaseth himself, the more is he exalted. 'To lose the head' is either to die or to go mad.
[2] I.e., who drinkest wine out of cups of gold. Addressed to the King.
[3] I.e., fair one
[4] 'Terah', Abraham's father, whom Muslims fable to have been a maker of idols for sale and high in favour with Nimrod.
[5] Gheyatheddin, surnamed Uweis, one of the Ilkhani Sultans of Baghdad, A.D. 1356–74 King had apparently neglected the poet.

CCCCXLI

Hafiz (1325–1390)
Translated by John Payne

Though weak and broken-hearted, Grown old and gray am I,
When of thy face I mind me, Yet young and gay am I.

Thanks be to God, whatever   Of Him I sought I had;
Possessed of all my wishes, Without gainsay, am I.

Ee'n as my friends could wish me, Winecup in hand, upon
The throne of bliss abiding, In Luck's highway am I.

Good luck to thee, young rosebush! For that the nightingale
Become of the world's garden, Beneath thy spray, am I.

Erst of the world no knowledge   I had; but, schooled of grief
For thee, become the expert   Thou seest to-day am I.

Since upon me there lighted   Thine eyes' calamity
Assured 'gainst Fortune's mischief   And Time's affray am I.

Open the door of vision   Is to my heart become,
Since on the Magians' threshold   A dweller aye am I.

My fate unto the winehouse   Consigned me for all time;
Howe'er to this inclining   Or t'other way am I.

Not old by years and seasons   I am: the faithless Friend,
Like life, hath passed me over   And hence grown gray am I.

Last night God's grace bespoke me; Said, "Hafiz, fret no more;
"Thy warrant for forgiveness, Betide what may, am I."

(1901)

Lament

By Mulheed; born in Adrianople, o.b. 1538, at Constantinople

James Clarence Mangan

My drooping heart, well mayest thou mourn
    That Liberty is dead, and Courage!
That both are gone without return,
    That Hope exists no more for *our* age!
The magazines wherein of old
    The Great and Good piled up their storage
Of gallant feats, ensamples bold,
    Have crumbled down to dust in *our* age!
The stately Tree of Liberty,
    Which, when the storms of tyrant Power rage,
Might yet lend shelter to the Free,
    Is shrunken and decayed in *our* age! [1]
The fakir begs on every road; [2]
    The heart's wealth grows a worthless dowerage,
Because the mighty souls that glowed
    In ages past glow not in *our* age!
Hope thou no more of Man, Mulheed!
    The stars forefend, the Fates discourage
Heroic scheme and glorious deed
    Among the sluggish souls of *our* age!

(1838)

[1] It flourished elsewhere in other times, yet may be remembered hereafter for little better than giving occasion to an epigrammatic couplet by Marmontel—

    Ah, Liberté cherie! en vain on te poursuit;
    Partout on voit ton arbre et nulle part tes fruits.

    Ah, well beloved Liberty! in vain we seek thee, go where
    We may; thy Tree is everywhere, thy fruits, alas, are nowhere.

[2] Man is now but a fakir (a beggar) on the highways of the world.

Ghazzel by the Durweesh Fakrideed, of Klish.

Minneti Chudaye ei dil her duneh minnetum yok

James Clarence Mangan

I give God thanks for this, that I
   Am no low slipper-licker's debtor.
If Heaven itself were not so high
   I scarce could bear to rest its debtor.
A Dirweesh am I—nought beside—
   I might be worse, and may be better; [1]
But one thought swells my heart with pride—
   I am no man's tool and no man's debtor.
I am sleek and stout—my face is bright—
   No cares corrode, no vices fetter
My cushioned soul;—I snore at night
   But never yet was opium's debtor.
I love the stars, the sun, the moon,
   When Summer goes I much regret her,
But who holds Kaf [2] or robs Karoon [3]
   I don't much care—I'm not their debtor.
So writeth Maumoud Fakrideed
   In this his lay, or lilt, or letter,
Which he or she that runs may read,
   And be therefor perchance his debtor.

James Clarence Mangan's ghazals collected in *Early Journeys, Forgotten Logs: The Nocturnal Iris Anthology of Ancient Ghazals in English* (2022); edited by R. W. Watkins.

(1840)

James Clarence Mangan

[1] He was afterwards made Sheikh of one of Suleiman's Persian Convents.
[2] The mountain which surrounds the earth and contains the treasures of the Pre-Adamite Sultans.
[3] The *Core* of the Old Testament, whom the Mooslemin believe to have been a sorcerer, and to have amassed immense riches by means of his magical practices,

Mountain Sijos

Gareth Writer-Davies

Before Science

No-one knew (before science) the age of rocks, so legends grew.
Maybe thrones of mountain Gods, the ridges spread, like a skewed hand.
Old enough to remember when rivers flowed East; before Man.

Quarry

Villages, faraway towns are constructed from this mountain.
The quarry is now worked out, a mantlepiece of broken rock.
I sit down on an undressed stone, look back to where I came from.

Waun Fach

You're standing on the highest of the mountains, the broken trig
in the marsh, beneath your feet, remembering the guide book said
the summit was the most boring of all mountains. It's raining.

Sijo Novice

John Baglow

The first line comes from the air, flies round my head, lands in the ink.
A second follows, buzzing. It too ends up drowned in the drink.
A third soars: hawk, moon, whatever—too late, alas. It's all over.

Haiku

late April breezes
hot air balloons emerging
from her bubble wand

     — Joshua St. Claire

a tightly clenched fist
bracing against the sharp air
daffodil's first bud

     — Marcia Burton

the universe sends
inscrutable messages –
hail on the window

no place else to go –
one more washed up man-o-war
reaches the strand line

     — Jonathan Aylett

Just before late freeze,
a single apple blossom
peaking through the fog.

     — G. C. Parker

on a quiet lake—
a young boy in a rowboat
fishing for himself

As I drift away . . .
the whip-poor-will still proving
that he knows his name

deep in the forest
the roar of a low jet plane
'til silence roars back

     — Alex Lubman

tin trumpet of the
ivory-billed woodpecker
Messier 40

     — Joshua St. Claire

dandelion clock
with one puff she takes us back
to happier times

     — Jonathan Aylett

wind chimes say nothing
that you don't already know—
it's now, then it's not

     — Lynda Zwinger

On the quiet tide
a mini-burst of thunder:
boat motor waking

     — Danielle Woerner

thunderstorm warning
flash of the white undersides
of the linden leaves

tornado weather
pressing through a June evening
stand of daylilies

distant lightning strikes
even after all these years
the hills fill with light

     — Joshua St. Claire

Caught in a downpour
   the smell of balsam poplar
   as we dash back home

     — R. W. Watkins

a song sparrow's nest
in morning glory tangle—
shelter from the storm

when the storm passes
only the sound of leaf drip
and a tethered dog

— Alex Lubman

mariners' warning
even the heron pauses
to greet the sunrise

— Reid Hepworth

Over ancient stones
rises rosy-fingered dawn:
Solstice symmetry

— Danielle Woerner

cautiously watching
paddler embarks silently
sandpiper on shore

sitting on a log
in quiet contemplation
turtle sunbathing

— Reid Hepworth

nautical twilight
at the edge of the ocean
a sandpiper's song

— Joshua St. Claire

the line between sea
and sky blurred without effort—
pelicans coasting

what is it really
air and sky, seagulls bobbing
the rim of my hat

cool caress of shade
under the beach umbrella
all answers are yes

tides and gravity
debris becomes poetry—
seashells, falling stars

— Lynda Zwinger

Our aquatic past
        unearthing rounded beach rocks
        in the seafront yard

Hiding in plain sight,
some nettles find amnesty
amongst the foxgloves

— R. W. Watkins

Gray lichen on limbs
does not make the tree stronger
though it looks like stone.

— Vicki Wilson

So much depends on
a chrysalis glazed with dew
fixed to a plum twig.

Our cat is spellbound
by the house cricket's struggle
in the spider's web.

When I slow my pace
the path to the mountaintop
freshens with birdsong.

— Alex Lubman

Haiku Mind, Enlightenment, and R. H. Blyth

Three related essays by Jim Wilson

What is Haiku Mind?

In the ongoing discussions about English-language haiku (ELH) over the years, a lot has been written about a topic often referred to as 'haiku mind'. For haijin like James Hackett, 'haiku mind' is intimately connected to the Zen experience of an enlightenment moment, or *satori*. Others reject a strong connection to the Zen tradition, yet they will agree that haiku does offer an experience of a kind of intuitive insight that goes beyond words. Eric Amann, at one period in his haiku-writing, referred to haiku as a "wordless poem". I want to explore this idea of 'haiku mind'. In this brief essay I will contrast two views of the concept. The first view is found in *Seeds from a Birch Tree* by Clark Strand.

In *Seeds* there is a chapter with the title 'Haiku Mind'. Strand writes:

"When you count the syllables for a haiku on your fingers and select a season word, already you have touched the mind of Basho and all the other haiku poets of the past. How could it be otherwise than this? People ask me what Haiku Mind is, and I offer various explanations in accordance with the place and time, but the truth is, it is only this. A haiku is a seventeen-syllable poem on a subject drawn from nature. This is both the simplest explanation and the secret of the art." (Page 87)

A different view is found in Patricia Donegan's book called *Haiku Mind*. It consists of 108 haiku by 108 haijin, both in English and in translation from the Japanese, with Donegan's brief commentary on each haiku. In the 'Introduction' Donegan writes:

"I wanted to write this book to share the idea of 'haiku mind' – a simple yet profound way of seeing our everyday world and living our lives with the awareness of the moment expressed in haiku – and to therefore hopefully inspire others to live with more clarity, compassion, and peace. The root of haiku mind is found in the widely-known poetic form of haiku, a form of poetry that contains seventeen syllables in three phrases (5-7-5) in Japanese or usually three lines in English. A fine haiku presents a crystalline moment of heightened awareness in simple imagery, traditionally using a kigo or season word from nature. It is this crystalline moment that is most appealing. However, this moment is more than a reflection of our day-to-day life – it is a deep reminder for us to pause and to be present to the details of the everyday. It is this way of being in the world with awakened open-hearted awareness – of being mindful of the ordinary moments of our lives – that I've come to call 'haiku mind.'" (Page XI)

The contrast between the two writers is worth unpacking. For Strand, 'haiku mind' is based on the mind that is counting 5-7-5 syllables. The counting brings our mind into alignment with the haiku tradition as a whole. For Donegan, the counting is mentioned, but only in passing. She notes that in ELH haiku there are "usually three lines", but the counting itself is not highlighted or considered foundational for ELH. For Donegan, the point of haiku is to offer us a "crystalline moment of heightened awareness". These two views are not mutually exclusive, yet they represent different starting points. For Strand, the starting point is simply counting syllables on our fingers; that is the ground and the awareness out of which haiku grow. For Donegan, the ground of haiku is a 'crystalline moment' which is then put to paper. Other factors are secondary to this crystalline moment of heightened awareness.

The approach Strand uses makes 'haiku mind' immediately accessible to everyone who can count syllables on their fingers. Donegan's approach is dependent upon having an experience of heightened awareness. In other words, Donegan's approach is esoteric. How do you know you are having this moment of heightened awareness? And what makes it special? If I write a haiku and I am not in a moment of heightened awareness, does that mean that my haiku are no good? Is this idea of heightened awareness helpful when I am not feeling well, so that my mind is cloudy (perhaps I have a fever), but I still want to write haiku? From Strand's perspective, as long as I can count 5-7-5, I can access 'haiku mind'—even when I am sluggish, or sick, or irritable. For Strand, accessing 'haiku mind' is not esoteric; it is exoteric and publicly available.

Haiku and Enlightenment

An aspect of English-language haiku is the often-expressed view that there is a connection between a well-written haiku and enlightenment. This view crosses the formal/free-verse divide; meaning that you find this idea advocated by both formal and free-verse practitioners of English-language haiku (ELH). The ELH scholars and poets who have held this view are significant: R. H. Blyth, James Hackett (who learned this view from Blyth), Robert Aitken, Kenneth Yasuda, Gabriel Rosenstock and Patricia Donegan are a few that come to mind. It's not a universally held view. Some have pushed back against it. Yet it remains a significant presence in ELH. I have recently been re-reading some of this material, and subsequently I would like to now make a few comments about this topic:

• The word 'enlightenment' is very slippery. It resembles a word like 'freedom'. People mean very different things when they use these words. For this reason, it is not always clear what ELH practitioners who hold to the idea of *haiku enlightenment*—or that haiku leads to enlightenment, or that the haiku experience is in some way an enlightening experience—mean.

• Some who advocate for this idea talk of a dropping of the conceptual mind and directly experiencing the object of perception in its purity before conception and analysis arise. Patricia Donegan speaks this way, and uses the example of seeing an orange for the first time, free from the concept of orange or any associated mental obscurations. I think Gabriel Rosenstock also holds this view, but I'm not completely confident about that.

• Some who advocate for this idea talk about a 'leap' that the mind makes when a haiku contains a disjunction. The idea is that the two parts of a haiku create a gap, and it is the gap itself, or our experience of it, that gives rise to haiku enlightenment. This is one reason why some ELH poets are fixated on disjunction. Entire books and journals are devoted to this way of writing ELH, in the hope of generating this kind of experience.

• One of the things that strike me about the depictions of haiku enlightenment that I have come across is that they emphasize individual experience. That is to say that haiku enlightenment appears to be always about the individual poet or reader 'having' this experience. It is distinctive that there is never any mention of a larger social context.

• It is a paradox of the idea of haiku enlightenment that it seeks to access the non-conceptual through the use of words—words that are highly structured. I don't recall this paradox being discussed.

• Those who advocate for haiku enlightenment tend to see haiku that are not focused on this enlightenment experience as 'not really haiku'. Some are explicit about this. This marginalizes a lot of haiku. For example, if someone starts writing haiku about their daily life, what flowers are blooming in their garden, what they had for breakfast, etc., this does not rise to the level of a 'real haiku' from this enlightenment perspective. And what I call 'pithy sayings' haiku would also not qualify as 'real haiku'. This idea of haiku enlightenment seems to grant those who hold the idea the right to determine who is writing 'real haiku' and who is not, based on their own view.

• The direct experience of things free from concepts and mental fabrications is something that people experience fairly often. It happens spontaneously when, to pick just one example, people engage with nature. It happens when listening to music. And it can happen while playing sports. This is accepted by those advocating for haiku enlightenment. But what I want to highlight here is that the idea that this experience is 'enlightenment' seems a stretch. It is a pleasing experience and it has significance. But in some ways I would argue that it is an ordinary experience. In Buddhist Abhidhamma the meditative absorptions are classified into eight types, four worldly and four trans-worldly. From what I have read, I would place the haiku enlightenment experiences in the second meditative absorption; because a distinctive feature of this absorption is the dropping away of mental labeling and conceptualization. From a traditional Buddhist perspective, that isn't enlightenment, if by enlightenment one means full realization in Buddhist terms. There are six more (higher) absorptions, each of them more rarefied, on the path to enlightenment.

• Japanese haiku poets do not seem to be inclined to embed haiku into this category of haiku enlightenment.

• The experience of haiku enlightenment, from what I have read, is depicted in worldly terms. I mean by this that it seems to be concerned with the things of this world and deepening our sense of their presence. This contrasts with traditional Japanese haiku, which is embedded in the flow of the seasons. From this perspective, the haiku experience is a type of transcendence that sees the objects of this world as flowing from invisible energies that give rise to these objects. The traditional haiku experience is a step into the beyond, beyond the sensory that gives rise to the sensory.

    • There is another way of looking at haiku and why it is satisfying and rewarding. That other way is 'haiku as craft'. From the perspective of haiku as craft there is a feeling of accomplishment in writing a haiku that accords with tradition. It is the same sense of accomplishment that a cook has when successfully completing a recipe. It is the same sense of accomplishment as when a gardener gathers the blossoms from the plants cultivated months before. It is the same sense of accomplishment that a quilter has when designing a quilt they plan to give to a friend. There may be other rewards in writing haiku; I suspect there are, particularly a gentle sense of transcendence. But the rewards of crafting words into a meaningful form, such as haiku, seem to me to be sufficient.

Poetry and Zen: A New Book about R. H. Blyth

I'm reading a new book, published this year, about R. H. Blyth. The book is *Poetry and Zen: Letters and Uncollected Writings of R. H. Blyth*, edited by Norman Waddell, the great translator of East Asian poetry and Buddhist works. The book collects previously unpublished letters and writings. The first part of the book is a biography of Blyth by Waddell; I found it very well written.

    R. H. Blyth had an enormous impact on haiku in the anglosphere, both on formal haiku and free-verse haiku. From the formal haiku perspective, it was Blyth's four volumes of haiku translations—with commentary—that brought both James Hackett and Richard Wright to haiku. I'm confident that others were similarly inspired.

    Here are a few tentative observations, or takeaways, or thoughts about Blyth and his legacy:

    • Blyth linked, or I might say 'entangled', Zen and Haiku, and this has had a big impact on how haiku is understood in the anglosphere (I'm not sure about other regions). In Japan, haiku is not linked to Zen in this way; but, because of Blyth, many people see haiku as an expression of Zen. But Blyth's understanding of Zen is, from my perspective, eccentric. Blyth is famous for stating that where institutional Zen differs from haiku, that Zen must defer to haiku. I'm not sure exactly what that means, but it is a clear statement of Blyth's priorities.

    • When I read Blyth's biography and his letters, as well as his published books, it is clear to me that the world Blyth inhabited was what I think I can call 'high culture'. He was linguistically skilled, he played multiple musical instruments, had a great love for J. S. Bach and classical music in general, and was ensconced in academia for most of his adult life. I think that is the source for how some people view haiku as a refined (I almost said 'elite') practice. I don't think Blyth intended that; but he equates Zen not only with haiku, but with upper echelon literary culture (he wrote a whole book about Zen in Western literature). This is partly mitigated by Blyth's interest in senryu, which I think he saw as a more popular expression. But he separates haiku and senryu into two different regions. In contrast, one of the things that has

R. H. Blyth, 1953

happened in popular haiku in English is that the distinction between haiku and senryu has dissolved.

• Clark Strand once said that the word "'haiku' is not a value judgment; it is a form." My feeling is that Blyth saw haiku as a value judgment; and that is part of his legacy to English-language haiku, and I think this has created a barrier to accessing haiku for some people.

• Blyth was a very interesting guy. He had a huge impact on how we understand haiku, but he was also very involved in the post World War II political sphere. Blyth was interned in Japan during the war (along with Robert Aitken), but immediately after became liaison to Emperor Hirohito and tutor to Akihito, the Emperor's son. In this position Blyth played a direct role in shaping postwar Japan.

Overall, I find Blyth's a complicated legacy. This new book about him highlights these complexities and gives us new insights into his work and life.

Senryu (or Haiku in a Lighter Vein)

Capitulation—
having to hire someone
to rake last year's leaves

Refugee babies
relaxing in their strollers
– American spring

— James Lignori

how delicately
the new mother cradles it
her Apple iPhone

family photos
my cell phone mimics the sound
of a shutter snap

a new string of pearls
how she smiles as his kisses
slowly creep downward

— Joshua St. Claire

Love on a gurney
We hear the monitor beep,
your heart skip a beat

— Danielle Woerner

one final item
added to my bucket list:
fix this leaky roof

$2/3$ H_2O...
in the next life I might be
a cumulous cloud

— Jonathan Aylett

About The Contributors...

Faiza Anum teaches literature in English at the University of Lahore, Lahore, Pakistan. She has published poems in various international magazines and journals, including *Transnational Literature* (Australia), *Illumen* (USA), *The Lake* (UK), and *Open Road Review* (India). Her poem 'Travelling Tales' was one of the finalists for the *Open Road Review* Poetry Prize of 2015.

Jonathan Aylett has spent periods as an ecologist, explosive ordnance disposal technician, and seafarer. Published in several journals and blogs, his style is traditionally structured haiku with a modern twist. He currently resides in Liverpool, England.

John Baglow is a writer living in Ottawa. He has appeared in many literary magazines over the years, and has published two collections of poetry (*Emergency Measures*, Sono Nis Press, 1976, and *Journey Under Glass*, Penumbra Press, 2004) and one book of literary criticism (*Hugh MacDiarmid: The Poetry of Self,* McGill-Queen's University Press, 1987).

Marcia Burton is a certified teacher of Mindful Self-Compassion and a senior Hakomi trainer and practitioner. She resides on Salt Spring Island in British Columbia.

Elias John Wilkinson Gibb (1857–1901) was born in Glasgow, at 25 Newton Place, to Elias John Gibb and Jane Gilman. He was educated by Collier and matriculated from Glasgow University in 1873. Gibb acquired a knowledge of Arabic and Persian languages, and became especially interested in Turkish language and literature. Gibb married and moved to London in 1899. He made a few visits to Europe, but never visited the regions that he studied. He did, however, come to be viewed as a sympathetic and talented orientalist, possessed an excellent library, and was acquainted with Muslim poets and scholars. His series of volumes on Ottoman poetry is especially noteworthy. He died aged 44 at his residence in London from scarlet fever, and was buried at Kensal Green Cemetery. His library was acquired by Cambridge University, the British Museum, and the British embassy at Constantinople. His name is commemorated in the long-running Gibb Memorial Series of publications. Funded by the trust established by Jane Gibb (d. 1904), the author's mother, the series is devoted primarily to the translation of Turkish, Persian and Arabic texts.

Hafiz or (more popularly in modern times) *Hafez* was the pen name of Khwaje Shams-od-Din Moḥammad Ḥafeẓ-e Shirazi (ca. 1325–1390), generally regarded as the greatest of all classical Persian poets.

Reid Hepworth lives in a tiny cabin in the woods in Jordan River, British Columbia, where she plays tiny ukulele and writes tiny poetry.

Mace Hosseini is a retired professional engineer whose avocations include painting and writing poetry. His e-book of poems and paintings, *The Lessons of the Soul*, is available from Amazon.com. He resides in LaSalle, Ontario.

Walter Leaf (1852–1927), son of Charles John Leaf, silk and ribbon dealer, was educated at Harrow, where Dean Farrar made him head of his house. Elected a classical scholar by Trinity College, Cambridge, he was bracketed Senior Classic in 1874 and became a fellow the next year. However, his father falling sick, he felt himself obliged to resign academic work and enter the family business. Later he turned to banking, and in 1918 became chairman of the London and Westminster Bank. Throughout his busy life he never deserted his original love, and attained high distinction as a Homeric scholar. He was a gifted linguist, and Persian was but one of many learned diversions.

James Lignori taught high-school English for 34 years, and is the recipient of the N.Y. State's English Council's Excellence in Teaching award. He is an active member of Hudson Valley Haiku-kai, a group of poets that meet to share and discuss their haiku poems.

Alex Lubman is retired from West Virginia University (libraries, tobacco cessation) where he also studied History and Musicology. He loves his wife and children, playing chamber music (viola), and writing and reading poetry. He lives under trees outside of Morgantown, WV.

James Clarence Mangan (1803–1849) was born at Fishamble Steet, Dublin, the son of grocer James Mangan and Catherine Smith. He was educated at a Jesuit school, where he learned Latin, Spanish, French, and Italian. Obliged to find a job in order to support his bankrupt parents, for seven years he worked as a scrivener's clerk, and for three years as a solicitor's assistant. He was later an employee of the Ordnance Survey and an assistant in the library of Trinity College, Dublin. Mangan's first verses were published in 1818. From 1820 onward he used the middle name 'Clarence'. In 1830 he began producing translations—generally free interpretations rather than strict transliterations—from German, a language he had taught himself. Of particular interest are his translations of Goethe. In 1837 he began producing translations from Turkish, Persian and Arabic for *The Dublin University Magazine*. He was also known for literary hoaxes; many of his 'translations' are in fact works of his own. After several years of contributions, his connexion with *The Dublin University Magazine* was terminated because his habits rendered him incapable of regular application. His relationship with patriotic Irish newspaper *The Nation*, for whom he would write poems in exchange for a fixed salary, would suffer a similar outcome. Most of his early poetry was apolitical, but after the Famine he began writing patriotic poems, including influential works such as 'Dark Rosaleen' (a translation of 16th century Irish lyric 'Róisín Dubh') and 'A Vision of Connaught in the Thirteenth Century'. In the last months of his life he wrote a brief autobiography, on the advice of his friend Charles Patrick Meehan, which ends mid-sentence. Mangan was a lonely and often difficult man who suffered from mood swings, depression and irrational fears, and became a heavy drinker and opium user. He was described by the artist William Frederick Wakeman as frequently wearing "a huge pair of green spectacles", padded shirts to hide his malnourished figure, and a hat which "resembled those which broomstick-riding witches are usually represented with". Weakened by poverty, alcoholism and malnutrition, he succumbed to cholera at age 46. He was buried in Glasnevin Cemetery, Dublin.

'Izzet Molla (or Kececizade Izzet Molla, as he is known in contemporary times) was a Turkish poet reputedly born Mehmed Izzet in 1786. His best known work is probably his humourous and autobiographical *Mihnetkesan* (1823–24), an epic poem written in the masnavi (or *mathnawi*) form and considered by many to be among the first works of modern Ottoman literature. Molla died in 1829.

Muhibbi was the pen name of Suleiman I (1494–1566), commonly known as Suleiman the Magnificent; the tenth and longest-reigning Sultan of the Ottoman Empire, reigning from 1520 until his death in 1566.

G. C. Parker (a.k.a. 'Bubba') is a retired technical supervisor (medical) who enjoys reading, cooking, and writing the occasional poem. He also enjoys making, restoring and collecting fountain pens. He lives in North Central Florida with his wife, two dogs and two cats.

John Payne (1842–1916), born in Bloomsbury, at the age of 13 moved with his parents to Bristol. He passed his early years as a clerk and an usher, but before reaching 19 he had made verse translations of Dante, Goethe, Calderon, and Lessing. He was an amazing self-taught linguist, and his numerous publications, many privately printed, include translations of the *Arabian Nights*, Villon, Omar Khayyam, Boccaccio, Bandello, and Heine; he also wrote several volumes of original poetry. He was a hotly controversial figure, his admirers praising him extravagantly; for all that he is not noticed in the *Dictionary of National Biography*. His style exhibits the extreme tendencies of Victorian neo-Gothic.

J. F. Shahrukh is a poet from Pakistan. This is his first published ghazal.

Joshua St. Claire is a married father of three young boys and an accountant by trade. He has some tanka and haiku forthcoming from *Scifaikuest*, a journal of science-fiction short poetry.

Alison Stone has published six full-length collections: *Caught in the Myth* (2019), *Dazzle* (2017), *Masterplan* (a book of collaborative poems with Eric Greinke, 2018), *Ordinary Magic* (2016), *Dangerous Enough* (2014), and *They Sing at Midnight*, which won the 2003 Many Mountains Moving Poetry Award; as well as three chapbooks. Her poems have appeared in *The Paris Review*, *Poetry*, *Ploughshares*, *Barrow Street*, *Poet Lore*, and many other journals and anthologies. A licensed psychotherapist, she has private practices in NYC and Nyack.

R. W. Watkins is the creator and editor of *Contemporary Ghazals* and *Eastern Structures*. His latest solo works are the haiku collection *Insight* and the essays collection *Exposing the Emperor, Consoling the Harem*.

Jim Wilson is a former Buddhist monk and prison chaplain. He currently runs a spiritual book and tea shop in northern California. He is also a member of a local Quaker group. A dozen books of poetry to his credit, Wilson has a strong interest in syllabic forms, which is the focus of his *Shaping Words* blog. In yet another existence, Wilson was better known as Tundra Wind, the creator and publisher of *APA-Renga*—or *Lynx*, as incoming editor Terri Lee Grell renamed it—the world's first English-language journal dedicated to the Japanese linked-verse form.

Vicki Wilson is a poet, playwright and novelist who resides in New York. She can be found at @wilsvick on Twitter.

Danielle Woerner published her first collection, *I Never Promised You a Cherry Orchard: Japanese short-form poetry, served with a Twist* (Sunrise Song Press), in July of 2021. Her haiku and senryu have been published in the arts and culture magazine *Chronogram*, and the *Three Nations Anthology: Native, Canadian & New England Writers* (Resolute Bear Press, 2017), as well as in *Eastern Structures*. Her features and op-ed pieces have appeared in *Classical Singer*, *New Music Connoisseur*, *Hudson Valley Magazine* and *Newsweek*, and she was a regular writer for the *Woodstock (NY) Times*. Her reporting for weekly newspapers in Maine was recognized in 2018 by the National Federation of Press Women. Woerner, also a BMI-affiliated songwriter, joined the Hudson Valley Haiku-kai in 2013.

Gareth Writer-Davies is a gardener from Letchworth, Hertfordhire, UK. His poems have appeared in such magazines as *Poetry News*, *The Journal*, *Bare Fiction* and *The Delinquent*. He was shortlisted for the Bridport Prize and the Erbacce Prize in 2014, and also highly commended in the Wallace Stevens Memorial Award in 2012 and 2013. He currently resides in Brecon, Powys, mid-Wales.

Lynda Zwinger has contributed to the Kyoto x Haiku Project and regularly participates in the Tricycle Haiku Challenge. She resides in Tucson, Arizona.